Puck
Farkinson's

Charleston, SC
www.PalmettoPublishing.com

Puck Farkinson's
Copyright © 2023 by Mike Justak

All rights reserved

No portion of this book may be reproduced, stored in a retrieval system, or transmitted in any form by any means—electronic, mechanical, photocopy, recording, or other—except for brief quotations in printed reviews, without prior permission of the author.

Hardcover ISBN: 979-8-8229-2639-4
Paperback ISBN: 979-8-8229-2236-5

PUCK FARKINSON'S

A Parkinson's Memoir

MIKE JUSTAK

For Karen,
My Inspiration,
My Joy,
My Life,
My Love.
Forever.

Cinema Verité

Have you ever been shuffling through Facebook and seen one of those *thought-provoking* questions? The kind of question that has you think back? The type of question seeking to explain some hidden life meaning? Is it just a silly game, or can it hold deeper meaning?

The questions may look like one of these.

If your life could be told by a song's lyrics, what song would you choose?

If your life were a sitcom, which one would it be?

If your life was portrayed as a twentieth-century movie, which one would that be?

JOURNEY

A *journey* is defined as travel from one place to another, usually over a long distance or time. There appear to be several tomes written about Parkinson's disease that are about a journey. However, a collection of stories offering detail about one's life should surely demand a more colorful adjective than journey. For instance, it could be epic. It could be an adventure. How about a pilgrimage? My jaunt with Parkinson's. My life's odyssey living well with Parkinson's disease.

Odyssey

I will embark on an odyssey, a Parkinson's odyssey. However, we will begin with a different odyssey. It was 1968, and my dad and I were about to take an adventure together. Just the two of us. We were headed to Chicago. The ticket read "Michael Todd Theatre Annex." It was the Cinerama presentation of *2001: A Space Odyssey*. We had reserved seats. The theatre was opulent, with red velvet drapes on red walls. Deep red carpet. We sat, and only a few minutes later, the curtain opened but just partially, and the overture began. The music was unusual and strange to say the least. The music faded; the screen was black. The house lights dimmed. What can best be described as a hum sound was played. As the view of Earth from space grew larger, the curtain opened to reveal its full width, while the drums banged out Bum! Bum! Bum! Bum! Bum! Bum! BUMMMMM!!!

"This is so cool!"

"Thanks, Dad. This is going to be great!"

To say the least, the film blew me away. Did I understand it? Hell no. This would become the only chance I would have to see the film projected in full-form Cinerama. Over the next twenty years, I would see it in theatres twice, on network TV once, and twice on Turner Classic Movies. It was a definite favorite. If you haven't seen it, here is the lowdown.

The film *2001: A Space Odyssey* begins with a prologue set in prehistoric Africa, where a group of apelike creatures discovers the use of tools after encountering a mysterious black monolith. The film then cuts to the twenty-first century, where a team of astronauts is sent on a mission to Jupiter to investigate another black monolith that has been found there. The mission is led by Dr. Dave Bowman, who is accompanied by Dr. Frank Poole and three other astronauts, who are in suspended animation.

The journey to Jupiter is uneventful, but things start to go wrong when HAL, the ship's computer, begins to malfunction. HAL reveals that he has become self-aware and that he is planning to kill the crew. Bowman manages to disable HAL, but not before HAL kills Poole. Bowman then continues on to Jupiter alone, where he encounters the second black monolith.

The monolith transports Bowman to a strange, otherworldly realm, where he undergoes a series of transformations. He eventually reaches a state of pure being, where he is able to see the universe as a single, unified whole. Bowman then returns to Earth, where he is reborn as a star child.

The name HAL is sort of an inside gag. Each letter is one removed from IBM. International Business Machines (IBM) was practically a monopoly in the early 1960s. I am of the thought that the monolith was both a developmental apparatus as well as a sort of security alarm. You can even think of it as a space GPS. Take a second and try to recall if you ever found a new tool. A tool that transforms your life. Do you find yourself looking over your shoulder as you believe you are being guided to an outcome?

* * *

2001 was almost as memorable an outing as our annual pilgrimage to the Chicago Auto Show each February. Later when the leaves turned, it meant one thing. Saturday was reserved for Notre Dame football. Dad was a season-ticket holder. They used to say being on the season-ticket-holder list would grant you eternal life because if you changed the name of the ticket holder, you would lose your tickets, and they would be sold to the person next in line. In time I would've hoped that was true.

The family's connection to the university was special. My dad's brother was a Holy Cross Brother. Their order held various positions at the university. I would spend the day with my uncle, Brother Reginald, while Mom and Dad watched the game. We would walk all over the campus. We'd go to the bookstore. Later we would check out the campus Knights of Columbus to grab a grilled steak sandwich. After that we would check out the basilica, grotto, and the log chapel. The chapel is where Mom and Dad were married.

To reflect on my life involves telling the story of how I came to believe that occurrences in life happen for a reason. Things or situations you encounter return later in life. It seems as if, at times, I am being guided to a result. Therefore, join me. Let me enlighten you on my life and, more importantly, how I navigated through twenty of my sixty-five years with Parkinson's disease. Sometimes the guidance is circular—kind of *déjà vu* in reverse.

• • •

Most simply put Parkinson's is a movement disorder. It's a progressive neurological disorder that has no cure. Its symptoms include tremors, stiffness and rigidity, loss of vocal volume, loss of balance, memory problems, cramped handwriting, and an unsteady gait. Even more simply put, Parkinson's sucks. It is possible to live a full life. It most likely will not be the life you planned and will bombard you with new outcomes from your everyday activities. Remember that things DO happen for a reason. Open your eyes. Open your mind. My life is far from mundane. It isn't a journey but rather an odyssey.

WAKE UP!

It was sunny but cold as we entered the basilica for the 4:00 p.m. Easter Sunday Mass—not our usual time for Mass time or church. Karen, my wife, had been upset that she had to miss Easter Mass because of work. I did some digging and discovered there was a late-afternoon Mass at the Basilica of St. Mary's in downtown Minneapolis. When I told Karen about it, she asked if I would be joining her. She felt it would be a good thing for me to attend, so I agreed.

I used to be a regular churchgoer, especially when the kids were young. The "kids" are my four children. Two girls and two boys. I don't mind adding that if the boys had been first, we most likely would have been a family of four, not six. Just kidding, guys. So, I introduce to you, in order of appearance, Katherine, Lauren, Ryan, and Greg. They arrived in two groups of two with six years in between. I never thought a family of six was unusual or large, but the looks we received when dining out told me different. I recall that when they were toddlers it was rather difficult to keep them attentive during Mass. At the time of my diagnosis, they would be twenty, eighteen, twelve, and ten years of age. It is ironic that now I am the one with the attention problem.

After my diagnosis I began taking a drug that had the side effect of inducing sleep. It could be a little embarrassing to begin to snore at the midpoint of the priest's homily. Karen was worried about me. You might say I was at a crossroads of sorts. My career was in the self-storage industry—you know the places with all the garages to put stuff in. More specifically I was in operations as a district manager. It was March 2006, and the company I worked for was about to be acquired by its rival in what is called an unsolicited, unfriendly takeover. The thing was that I had worked for that company for seven years—seven long years. I was not happy to be dining at their table once again. I did not plan on staying there long. However, I needed to stay until January 1 to receive my bonus. This year

I was on track to almost double my take-home pay with this bonus opportunity and had been told the new company would honor it.

Looking at a company culture is like looking at a photo and its negative. Take healthcare for example. Here I quote the HR person speaking at a get-to-know-us meeting: "Your CEO has the same health plan as the frontline counter person. Here at company *Big Guy*, we don't offer anything to employees below district manager." Let's compare the cultures. Current: encourage employee ownership. Future: screw employee for every dime.

This *crossroad* was one of those *markers* in life. You could call it a milepost. Those big moments you remember, such as first day of school, graduation, marriage, children, loss of a parent, or illness.

You hope they stay in their normal order. Some you hope come as late in life as possible. Others you greet with joy. When the order is upended, it feels like a punch to the gut. For me the gut punches would begin too early, the most noteworthy at age fifteen. Life isn't easy. You can't stay down; you have to get up and fight.

It's 2006. I'm in Church for Easter Mass, and I'm at a Crossroad.

We arrived at the basilica at about 3:50 p.m. for the 4:00 p.m. Mass.

We opened the heavy wooden door and began walking to our seats. You could hear the echo of the clop-clop our shoes made against the granite floor.

As Mass began, I was feeling ok. The entrance hymn was beautiful, but it was Easter, and they began to sing the parts of the Mass that are normally spoken. I started to tune out. I was thinking about those mileposts—how I was growing an impressive contact list. What could I do next? As the gospel concluded, we sat. I was hardly able to stay awake. My head was jerking down and then up. Down, then up. Down, then up. Down, then up. Down, way down.

I snapped up and was alert. I could see images—hundreds, no thousands of images. Scrolling by, then flashing. Beautiful. A rainbow of colors. They were vivid images of me, my family, my home, my parents, and people I worked for and with. I was dumbfounded. Utterly amazing! One of the images seemed to repeat, then linger a little longer. And then WHAM—the last image faded to white and was gone. I turned to Karen, who was staring intently at me. I looked at her and whispered, "Michael J. Fox. Remind me. Michael J. Fox."

I was fully awake, but my mind was open like a blank canvas. I stayed that way until the Mass concluded. We both sat down in the pew. Karen spoke first.

"Mikel, what happened?" (Say Michael but spell M-I-K-E-L.) This is why I never liked roll call at the start of a new school year.

I explained how I was thinking about my job and that I was falling asleep. "About the midpoint of the homily, my closed eyes opened wide. I saw all these images. They were all from my life, except for one. The image of Michael J. Fox."

• • •

Karen's response was utterly intuitive. We had talked about how it would be nice to work in the Parkinson's field. The Michael J. Fox Foundation was just a few years old, so it seemed like a good place to look. "Mikel, you have been looking for guidance. Unsure of what to do. You are here, in this beautiful church, on Easter Sunday! A day of fresh starts. A day of new beginnings. You asked for guidance, and it has been given."

All I could say was, "Shazam."

We exited and returned to our car for the trip home. The family was waiting for our return so we could enjoy Easter dinner together. We entered through the garage and heard the family. The TV was on. I looked over at the screen and *Dateline NBC* was on. They were doing a story on Muhammad Ali. His wife, Lonnie, was speaking about how they believed things in life all happen for a reason. They went to a commercial, and a new story began after the break. This story was about a young Canadian who, at the peak of his career—he wasn't even forty years old—was doing battle with Parkinson's disease.

Michael J. Fox.

Shazam!

DIAGNOSIS

The year 2004 would be one of firsts and new experiences. The new national storage company that bought out the Minnesota partnership was about to hand us a new regional director. He was a rather unique guy who was overqualified to be a regional, so it was a very lucky opportunity to learn from him. Later in the year, I would have my first appointment to meet with a neurologist to discuss some peculiarities I was experiencing. And before Thanksgiving I would have my first trip to Rochester, home of the Mayo Clinic.

For a newcomer walking into the Mayo Clinic is really something to see. I would say they are the NASA of medical diagnostics. You are given an itinerary of what will happen and when and where. This was day two for me. The diagnostics were complete, and we were going to have a consult with the neurologist. Just what I wanted or needed—some doc telling me my brain was screwed. It was November 2004, not unusually cold. This was Minnesota after all. As we walked into the meeting room, I could hear my heart pounding. I reached for Karen's hand. She, in turn, reached to meet my hand and then held it tightly. Seconds later there was a knock, followed by the doctor's entrance. He started by reviewing the testing. He talked about the physical tests. I reran them in my mind. "Tap your left foot. Tap your right foot. Hold your arms straight out. Quickly move your right wrist left to right and back. Do the same with your left wrist." The wrist turn reminded me of how this all began. I couldn't brush my teeth. I started normally, but then my arm just stopped working.

The doctor looked directly at me.

"Young Onset Parkinson's disease."

"What the ***k is that?"

• • •

The rest of the meeting was a blur. The drive home was quiet.

I didn't like that Mayo doctor.

• • •

We started looking for anything we could find on Parkinson's disease. Most articles just regurgitated the same info. At best treatments helped ease symptoms. You should recall the list of symptoms was long; however, Parkinson's was like a designer disease. Every person would be different from the other patients. The symptoms could include: physical tremors, stiffness, rigidity, lack of arm swing, balance difficulty, memory issues, constipation, trouble sleeping, cramped handwriting, and lack of facial emotion. Geez, this list sounds like the side effects listed in one of those TV drug ads.

It usually occurs when someone is over sixty; one in five will be younger than fifty.

No known cure.

We searched for a doctor close to home. It wasn't practical to make two-and-a-half hour drives to Mayo. We stumbled upon a clinic ten minutes away. They specialized in the treatment of Parkinson's. The head of neurology was even accepting new patients.

"Ok. Let's make the appointment."

There was another matter to deal with. The tell.

Karen was ready to announce to the extended family what I was dealing with. That struck a nerve. "No. Don't tell anyone."

"Mikel," Karen said.

"No!"

I was entering a phase of denial. I wasn't sick. I didn't have that old folk's thing. It was none of their business.

Karen would appeal to me from time to time.

"Mikel, there is a group meeting. Patients like you."

"No. I don't need a lecture. Don't call me a patient."

I had placed Karen in the worst possible place. The stress she was feeling was terrible. The extended family knew we went to Mayo. They noticed I walked funny—that I struggled eating the lettuce in my salad. It was a difficult period. She honored my request. It was now March 2006, and my world was about to have an A-bomb dropped on it. The world's largest self-storage company just made a bid to take over our company. As I earlier said, I had worked for them seven years earlier. I did not want to go back. The takeover offer was too good to pass on. Investors would be rewarded handsomely. I was going to need a new job. And I still had the tell hanging over my head.

I was thinking that I was being selfish. I didn't want to keep the secret any longer.

It was almost Easter Sunday. "Let's selectively start informing everyone about what I am facing."

Does Guidance Come with Cliff Notes?

The events of Sunday stayed with me as I returned to work. Work was a sort of in limbo as transitioning was starting to emerge. There were quite a few meetings. The more I heard, the less I wanted to be there. The talk was that the takeover would be complete by the end of August. That meant I needed four months to collect my bonus. Surely, I could last that long. Just prior to the merger, the Minneapolis team went to Red Lobster for lunch. We were standing next to the lobster tank when my counterpart, Joe looked at the lobsters and posed the question, "What do you think they are thinking?"

I said, "You think we have it bad—those four have to go work for Big Guy storage."

The more I thought about it, the more I felt compelled to contact the Michael J. Fox Foundation. I had been researching contact info and decided to write one letter addressed to Mr. Fox, a copy to Debi Brooks (the foundation CEO), as well as a copy to the director of development. In the letter I wrote about the events of Easter as well as the crossroads that I was on. I mailed all three to the foundation address in New York City. Before I placed them in the mail, I decided to get an opinion from someone who I have great respect for and could call a mentor. His response was an overwhelming yes to mailing them. Several times he repeated, "You have to mail this!" So, I plopped them into outgoing mail at the Plymouth post office. Four weeks later in early June, I had received no answer to my letters. I came to a decision that I had misread the tea leaves and would rethink my future, as I had obviously made a mistake. I stepped outside to retrieve the morning newspaper. I opened it to do a quick check of the news, and my jaw dropped when I saw the op-ed column. It was a piece on the subject of Parkinson's disease. So now I was thinking I was giving up too easily. I wrote a second letter tied to the op-ed piece in the *Minneapolis Star Tribune*. I again recalled the events of Easter Sunday, and I once again sent letters to Michael and Debi. I again addressed them to the foundation's New York City address. Days passed. Again! Days became weeks. It was early September. On the career front, I was under *new management* or rather under *old* management. It was a hard day, and I was a little depressed. When I arrived home, I stopped at the mailbox per my usual. There was lots of mail that day. Let's see—AARP—I always hated that one. *Star Tribune*. Michael J. Fox Foundation for Parkinson's Research, City of Plymouth. Hello!

It was a letter from Fox. I threw the car into park and ran inside so Karen could read it with me.

It wasn't a reply but an invitation. A scientific roundtable was to be held on October 28 in Chicago. CHICAGO! You see I grew up on the Indiana side of Chicago's East Side. This was better than a letter reply; I was going to get a face-to-face. I needed to mail one more letter. I would be available to interview. I needed a clever hook.

I had it. *The Blues Brothers*. This was perfect. I recalled that some twenty-plus years earlier, I was in a perfect position. I was standing in Chicago's Grant Park with two buddies when we heard this loud whoomp-whoomp sound. We turned in circles, trying to see the source. As we looked up, a large helicopter appeared, rising above the tree line. It had a cable or something hanging below. While it was still rising, we watched as a car appeared, suspended by the cable. The ascent stopped and then, in an instant, the car was released and plunged down. We ran as fast as we could, but it struck prior to our arrival. We looked and saw cameras, boom equipment, police cars, and the helicopter. All near Lake Shore Drive's S curve. They were filming a *Blues Brothers* scene. The scene involved Illinois Nazis in a car that jumps through a missing bridge sign and hurdles to the ground. Here is the synopsis for the movie if you haven't seen it.

THE BLUES BROTHERS

~~~

The central plot of *The Blues Brothers* is a tale of redemption for paroled convict Jake and his blood brother Elwood, who both set out on a *mission from God* to prevent foreclosure of the Roman Catholic orphanage where they were raised. To do so they must reunite their R&B band and organize a performance to earn the $5,000 needed to pay the orphanage's property tax bill.

The film opens with Jake Blues being released from prison after serving three years. He is picked up by his brother, Elwood, in his Blues mobile, a battered former police car. The brothers visit the Catholic orphanage and learn from Sister Mary Stigmata that it will be closed unless $5,000 in property taxes is collected.

Jake and Elwood set out to raise the money by reforming their old Blues band. They recruit their old bandmates.

The band sets out on a tour of Chicago, playing at various clubs and bars. They are pursued by the local police, the Illinois Nazis, and the state police.

Despite all of the obstacles, the Blues Brothers manage to raise the $5,000 and save the orphanage.

Now take a moment and think about this. I was undergoing a crisis; I had a vision of a solution at a church service. I needed to raise money to help others. I took the above and penned my third letter to the Fox trio.

It was a little *out there*, but you must admit, it was unique and creative. I am certain that very few people would use the movie *The Blues Brothers* to represent their life. In the letter I explained that I would be attending the scientific roundtable and willing to take time to meet on either side of it. I addressed the letter to the same Fox trio.

And waited.

"I wonder if I was a little too over the top?"

The point here is life doesn't just hand you something good. You need to persevere. You may need to go outside your comfort zone. You don't want to blend in. You want to stand out. The Blues Brothers? Heck yes!

Nights of the Roundtable

Without a reply to my letter, we boarded the flight to Chicago. We were prepared and armed with good, tough questions to ask the panel. I figured it was a good tool to make myself even more memorable. The questions came from the neurologists at the Struthers Parkinson's Center.

We arrived and took our seats near the head table of the roundtable. Karen and I had our question cards out on the tabletop. Debi Brooks was seated at the table, reviewing her notes by herself. This was my chance.

I took a breath and approached her.

"Ms. Brooks, may I have a minute of your time? My name is Mike Justak. This is my wife, Karen, and we came here today from Minneapolis."

"Minneapolis? You came all that way from Minneapolis?"

I thanked her for her work and what it meant to a person like myself, who had Parkinson's.

We exchanged a few pleasantries, and I returned to my seat. I could tell from her reaction that my name meant nothing to her. I was certain she had not seen any of my letters.

As the roundtable began, all Fox employees on hand were introduced, including Karen L., development director. At a break I approached her.

"Karen, hi. My name is Mike Justak, and this is my wife, Karen. We flew in from Minneapolis."

"Wow, you came all the way from Minneapolis?"

Don't you New Yorkers fly anywhere? It's a quick hop, I thought to myself.

Once again, I could tell she did not recognize my name. She hadn't read the letters. But with Karen I pressed on.

"Well, Karen, you know I authored three letters to you. Well, not actually you, but to Michael and a copy to you. In one of the letters, I told you about an awakening of sorts that I experienced on Easter Sunday."

"I have not seen this letter. I would have remembered such a thing. Where did you send it?" she asked.

"To your New York City office. It was addressed to Michael, with a copy to you."

"Oh, you should not have done that. Michael's mail is heavily screened. I would like to see it please. Here is my email and direct phone line, and here is the fax number."

I informed her of my intention to have them in her hands over the weekend.

We enjoyed the balance of the roundtable. About an hour later, we said our goodbyes. The next morning as we waited to check out, I heard, "Mike. Mike!"

It was Debi Brooks heading home.

She knew me. She remembered. She was on her way out and just wanted to wish us well. It made my day.

Four weeks later my phone rang. It was Karen L. I had begun to think she had changed her mind. I could not have been more wrong. She apologized for the delay, explaining that her largest fundraiser, "A Funny Thing," had just occurred. There was a colleague with her. They asked if I could be available to elaborate on my plans with them. We set a date for fourteen days out. We would do a conference call at 1:00 p.m.

Wonderful Life

Most people my age are probably very familiar with the movie *It's a Wonderful Life*. In a way it's funny because originally it wasn't very popular, until it fell into the public domain and every TV station on earth would run it for Christmas. Then Network Television secured the rights, bringing it back to a single showing a year. The themes of the movie seem to resonate with me. If you need a quick review, here you go.

It's a Wonderful Life is a 1946 American Christmas fantasy drama film produced and directed by Frank Capra. It stars James Stewart as George Bailey, a man who has given up his personal dreams in order to help others in his community and whose thoughts of suicide on Christmas Eve bring about the intervention of his guardian angel, Clarence Oddbody.

The film opens with George Bailey, a small-town banker, contemplating suicide on Christmas Eve. He has been feeling down, as he has been unable to fulfill his dreams of traveling the world and becoming an architect. He has also been feeling overwhelmed by the responsibility of running his family's savings and loan business, which is in danger of going bankrupt due to a missing payment to the bank.

Just as George is about to jump off a bridge, he is saved by Clarence, a guardian angel who has not yet earned his wings. Clarence shows George what life in Bedford Falls would have been like if he had never been born. In this alternate reality, Bedford Falls is a bleak and miserable place where people are poor, unhappy, and hassled by crime.

George is horrified by what he sees, and he realizes that his life has had a positive impact on the world. It is noted that the removal of even just one life leaves a large hole. He thanks Clarence for showing him the truth and vows to never give up on his dreams.

It's a Wonderful Life perfectly illustrates how the power of a single individual is able to triumph and influence others. It demonstrates how easy it can be for you to go to a dark place. Relating this to Parkinson's, you will have days where you are on the bridge. Do you have a Clarence on your support team? Is there a Mr. Potter lurking in your background? Life can interfere with dreams. Be prepared. You should know that stress is Parkinson's friend. It makes symptoms worse.

Life may just place a milepost in your path at an unexpected moment.

DIY

From time to time, I find myself recalling the events of the Fox interview. How your future can depend on a single question, not only on the words of your answer but on the confidence, you display with that answer. In this case it was my answer to the very first question.

"Is this a *paid* position you seek?"

I had never imagined that an interviewer could kill the interview with a single seven-word question. Undaunted I replied:

"Well, yes, it is. However, with the knowledge that we both know how this discussion will ultimately conclude, I would like to suggest we proceed so I can share my thoughts on what I can offer the foundation."

So, a phone call that should have lasted five minutes lasted just short of two hours. It was an opportunity to learn and grow my own boundaries. I had zero experience raising money. What

I lacked in skill, I made up for with creative, if not adventurous, ways to raise awareness and money. I like to think that it was my phone call that triggered an opportunity the foundation was overlooking—that of using volunteers to do fundraising across the country. They would call it Team Fox, and it was rolled out months later.

That same day I summarized events for a former colleague and mentor, who suggested, "If your ideas are really that good, why not start a nonprofit yourself?"

As I researched how to organize and establish a nonprofit, it was clear the burden would rest on my shoulder of competency. I would push the pencil and complete all the filing of needed forms.

I simply couldn't afford to hire professionals. The IRS 1023 was key. This form creates your status for tax exemption. It was $750 for each time you applied. I had to pass on the first try. I did just that. The stars were shining on me as far as my employment future also. I had been interviewing for a regional manager position with a new self-storage company that was growing aggressively.

The year 2007 could be renamed the year of *Don't know how to do it? Do it anyway.* I didn't know anything about organizing a new business, but I did it anyway. File IRS exemption status. I had never even seen a form, but I did it anyway. That August we received the IRS letter granting us 501c3 exemption status. The Mike Justak Foundation for Parkinson's Disease was born. We created a website at the address www.mjfpd.org.

On top of all of that, Karen and I were going to Atlanta. Our destination was the Early-Onset Parkinson's Disease Conference. A key to being successful in mitigating the effects of Parkinson's is staying current on developments with the disease. I attended a session on how the use of the Nintendo Wii game machine, combined with the balance board option, could be used as a rehab tool. Wii-Hab would offer clinical reports to demonstrate just how effective it could be. The boxing *game* was especially shown to help those with Parkinson's.

Another session was dubbed "Delay the Disease." This was an interactive class that used techniques and specific exercises to ward off Parkinson's. There was discussion on the importance of remaining social, as well as exercising your brain.

It was here I met David Zid. He authored the book *Delay the Disease*. He offered to take his show on the road to demonstrate firsthand how—when done daily—these few exercises could be an important contribution to improving your symptoms. I jumped at the opportunity to sponsor him for a Twin Cities demonstration.

LESSONS IN ATLANTA

The Atlanta conference was also able to illustrate how most people don't understand what Parkinson's is about.

There was a continental breakfast planned for that first day. Karen and I dressed and dashed over to the convention hall. The conference would begin with a general session this day. Outside the hall and lining the walls in between each set of entry door posts were tables complete with tall brew pots of coffee, decaf coffee, and hot water. Cups were stacked in groups of six high and ten across. There were storage bins that dispensed dry cereal and a push-button milk dispenser. It looked great—only one problem. People with Parkinson's don't have dexterity. They struggle with tremors and loss of balance. Now multiply that by four hundred. If somehow you managed to get that coffee, you then faced the long walk to your seat hundreds of feet away.

It was not just funny; it was hysterically funny and a huge miss on the part of the banquet manager. NOTE TO SELF: Allowing Parkinson's people to walk with coffee will require scheduling carpet shampoo/cleaning after the event. This banquet manager demonstrated that *people can be taught*. The next morning all the tables outside the hall were gone. Stations had been established within easy steps of the general session seating. Coffee pots sat on each table, as well as pitchers of milk and creamers. Order had been restored, as well as my faith in management to stand by their guests.

All in all, it was an uplifting few days that offered hope. For the first time, I was upbeat about facing this disease. I could tell that Karen emerged energized from the weekend as well. Yes, there is HOPE.

DAVID

Before I knew it, November had arrived. I tried my hardest to promote David's appearance, but his name was not known in the area, and neither was mine. I did manage to have a few of my new friends from the support group join in. All told we were able to bring twenty people together for David's symposium on exercise and how it affects Parkinson's disease. I was disappointed not to bring their usual one hundred or more attendees.

David asked everyone to stand. After ten minutes he had us sit. He asked if anyone had trouble standing up from a chair. A few raised their hands. David explained, "It can be quite easy, just like when you were ten, if you know the secret. First remember your balance is all out of whack. Instead of sitting to the back, reposition yourself as close to the front of the chair as you can get. Square off your legs at straight angles. Now pretend you are a steam shovel with your hands as the bucket. Center between your knees. Dig down to scoop and quickly rise up, pulling yourself up as well."

Everyone was standing. Everyone. Then a woman in the back corner started to cry. Everyone turned to look. Was she hurt in some way? David rushed over, and as he approached, she reached out to grab David and give him a huge bear hug. The startled David looked at her as she spoke. "It's been five months since I rose unassisted from a chair. Until today. You gave me a piece of my life back."

David hugged her back and returned to center stage.

Karen was crying. I was crying. Hell, the whole room was crying. I looked back at Karen.

"If I ever ask, why me, remind me of today," I said.

MCO MSP

I would restart my self-storage career with a new company. Six months later I became the director of asset management, my dream position. I would report directly to the owner. My office was next to his. However, it was in Orlando. Somehow, I was able to convince him to allow me to commute from Minneapolis. He didn't know my secret. My position involved extensive use of Microsoft Excel. Typing was difficult at times. I was using my left hand to mouse with, although I was right-handed. My work involved data analysis on 200-plus tabs in a single workbook. Add in the stress of the flights to commute and you can see something was going to clash.

Mr. K was the best person I could have worked for. I worked hard and was challenged daily. Kyle was house attorney and Mr. K's trusted friend. When the time was right, I would advise them of my medical dilemma. It wouldn't be long before I was ready to do just that.

One year later I was comfortable with my position, and I explained what was happening. A few weeks later we enjoyed dinner together. I had just returned from a visit with Dr. Nance, my neurologist, who prescribed a new medication. I told them that I was cautioned to be aware that a side effect could cause hallucinations. I asked them to make me aware of any strange behaviors they might notice. I thought things went very well.

As I walked into my hotel room, my phone rang. It was Kyle. He was checking to see if I had made it back and wasn't lost. I thought I'd have a little fun. "Hey, Kyle. How is it you were able to get Obama to join us?"

Kyle responded, "DUDE! You must have had a hallucination. That wasn't Obama, it was Oprah!"

Classic.

Mr. K was a great person to work with. He had high standards. He could think on his feet and would challenge you constantly. I really loved my job! By the fifth year it was obvious that I was not the same person that entered 4 years ago. The symptoms I encountered worsened. My productivity dropped. Mr. K was patient. I owed it to him to wrap things up as soon as possible.

My years with Mr. K were a reminder of the personal cost of this disease. I was going to be brain-jacked and denied the opportunity to maximize my income. Hey, life! I have four children to put through college. Planning helped me get through this. My healthcare was carried out by Karen's employer. I was covered by a disability policy that I paid the premiums for. These policies pay out federal tax-free if you pay the premiums. When combined with Social Security, the policy would equal 65% of my pre-retirement salary. My advice is to get all the insurance you can afford. Ask to see the policy so you can read it. Make note of definitions and calculations used to arrive at a defined point. Pay special attention to pre-existing condition language in the policy.

Reflections

I believe that a large part of your character originates from your upbringing. To help you gain some perspective, I offer a bit of introspective here. Yes, I believe boys follow their father's influence.

I am the youngest of three brothers.

My dad was in business with his twin brother.

We lived in an area more commonly referred to as *the region*.

The nickname reflected its badass reputation. Most everybody was connected to employment either in the steel mills or the oil refineries. The refineries would light the sky when the huge flare stacks would ignite. And when the wind was right, the sky was orange from the smoke from the steel plants. The beaches on Lake Michigan were closed due to water pollution. Not quite the healthiest place to grow up.

Here are few of my early recollections. I recall the weekend trips to Detroit on the new I-94

Expressway. There were the outings to Chicago and Sunday drives on the newest section of I-94 open to traffic. We loved Sunday picnics with neighbors or family at the Indiana Dunes or the Warren Dunes in Michigan.

I remember working the lighting crew for the eighth-grade talent show, a reflection of my interest in things electrical.

If you could go back in time to 1969 and talk to me about the future, you might be surprised. What was my future? Broadcasting. Broadcast engineering. I'm what some would call a geek. I was amazed by the TV coverage of the Apollo moon missions. I didn't want to be an astronaut, but I adored the TV coverage. How do they get pictures from the moon? The props used. Instant. Live via satellite.

There was my radio station, WJJJ. Three guys with last name initial J. I had purchased a real broadcast radio transmitter. No limits. I even climbed a telephone pole to mount the antenna. I was fearless at that age. Letterhead was printed with our BIG 60 logo. The studio was in the basement. I was able to get on mailing lists for promotional records by using the letterhead. Then one day records started to flow in. I would play the records for three buddies and then take a vote. A reply to the ad agent would read, "Sixty-three percent of the listening audience loved it!"

I spent countless hours on the studio design and construction. A DJ's paradise. Not just a DJ I was an electrical engineer too! Solder gun. No problem. I built my first stereo amplifier from a kit. What happened? Why the change? I grew up. I was in high school now and adjusting to a new school and classmates. The summer prior to the start of my freshman year, Dad strongly suggested that I not waste the summer and go to summer school and take classes in bookkeeping and typing.

I believe he hoped I would join him in his business, Justak and Sons. The family business was started by my grandfather and his sons. It was a trucking company that had true horsepower behind it. Occasionally I would go play in the barn that now housed trucks instead of horses and wagons as in the early days.

My dad was the accountant and ran the office. I recall times when he picked me up at school, and I went to the office with him, and we rode home together. On Saturday I would ride with dad to go to the cemetery. Stuff like that. I remember the August Sunday that Dad received the news that his brother, the brother, had collapsed while walking along a path in Chicago's Grant Park, succumbing to a heart attack. I would miss Brother Reginald. I should have thought more about those trips on Saturdays to the cemetery. Three brothers and their father had markers there. Their deaths eerily similar. All died in August. All died from heart attack. All died way too soon.

The year that followed saw many projects around the house. New roof on garage. New sidewalk, waterproofing in basement, and a new roof for the house.

Here we were in the final weekend of August already. It was just about a year since Brother Reginald had died. Another week and I would start my sophomore year. But today we headed for Detroit. Now pronounce it correctly.

First if you are from Chicago, it is pronounced Dee-troit. Just like if you are from Whiting, Indiana, you say Joo stack for Justak. Detroit was a summer destination. Dad had a Navy buddy that lived in Grosse Pointe Park. Each summer we took the new interstate on a four-hour drive to visit him. We usually stayed near the Fischer Building at the Harlan House Motor Inn. Detroit seemed like it could be a neat place to live. The sky wasn't orange either.

ALONE. AGAIN. NATURALLY.

The family was heading to Detroit for a wedding! My oldest brother, Mel's. I would ride in the car with my brother Gary driving the Olds Cutlass. Mom and Dad were in the Olds 98, and Mel was in his yellow Ford Torino. Detroit iron heading back to the Motor City.

It was hot that day and a little warm in the banquet hall. They were a little behind. I heard the announcement asking the parents to come forward for the first dance. Mom and Dad were pretty good dancers. As the dance concluded, Dad slipped from Mom's arm and collapsed onto the floor. Heart attack. He was gone just that quick.

Life became lifeless. Smiles vanished. Tears emerged. The cruelty of it. You are not supposed to think of family loss and grief at a wedding. I don't remember much other than the ride home. Four long hours. No air-conditioning in the car. I tried to sleep, but on the radio, there was that damn song playing. It seemed like it was the only song being played. I must have heard it twenty times during the drive. The song? "Alone Again Naturally." Listen to the words. "I remember I cried when my father died." I hate that song. I MEAN, I HATE THAT SONG. F*** you, Gilbert O'Sullivan. To this day I can't listen to it.

In the weeks that followed, Mom learned a lot. Mom and Dad had been old school. Dad was the provider. Mom took care of him, the boys, and the house. He gave her the budget allocation each week. She did not even know how much dad made. The attorney handling the estate was a Justak from Indianapolis. A blood Justak—Albert was Dad's twin brother. Mom was not blood. The valuation of the business was skewed to Albert we would discover. It would only take a few months to lose contact with those family members as the bickering continued. Within a year I never saw any family associated with Albert—uncles, aunts, cousins. Gone.

Nobody even called to say, "How you doing, Mike?"

Before you knew it, I had graduated from high school and entered the strange new world of college. I joined a social fraternity. Sigma Nu. The fraternity allowed competing behaviors to co-exist, that of leadership and that of immaturity. Hopefully as you progressed through your chosen school of learning, the immaturity lessened and the leadership grew. Fraternities often were labeled. Our label? We were a group of "smart asses." That wasn't necessarily a bad thing as you needed to think quickly to deliver an appropriate response when challenged. Sort of a debate-team mentality. The atmosphere in the fraternity house helped develop my spirit of competitiveness. For my junior year, I held the position of treasurer and applied for and won a seat on the Student Center Governing Board. Senior year I was elected president of our fraternity chapter. It was a challenging year to be the president. That summer had a breakout comedy film *Animal House*. The film depicted a fictitious fraternity more focused on the immature side of things.

I was called "Hoover," the happy-go-lucky president of the delta house in the film.

Speaking of immaturity, I established a new highpoint for Halloween costume back in my freshman year.

My costume fit my personality. I dressed as a Christmas tree. I wore a large green trash bag decorated with paper ornaments and a paper wreath. I had 500 indoor/outdoor twinkle lights that plugged in at my ankle and attached to a ten-foot extension cord. I knew where every outlet was, so I could stay plugged in. Every thirty minutes or so, I would stand in a corner and be serenaded to "O Christmas Tree." It was quite a scene. In May of 1979, I became the first Justak to graduate from college with a bachelor's degree. I took a position within my brother's trucking business—liquid waste removal to be exact. Two years later someone new joined the office staff. Karen.

I found the courage to ask her out on a date. She accepted! My pulse quickened near her. I wanted to talk with her. I wanted to hold her hand. Have her hold my hand. That first kiss was the most magical moment of my life. One year after we met for that first date, we wed.

It's funny how you can know someone for years without really knowing it. Karen is six years younger than I am, so our circles didn't quite overlap. We both went to the same elementary school. We attended the same church. My mother's sister, who is my godmother, lived just a few houses away from Karen's parents' house. Karen's uncle George is married to my godmother. Uncle George installed a hot water heater for my dad a few years back. Karen's dad, Joe, installed a tile floor in my mom and dad's house when I was seven or eight. Karen's dad was the custodian of the church. We did *know* each other actually. The age separation was large enough to make it seem as if we didn't.

My life had circles. People. Places. Events. It seemed an endless feeling of *déjà vu* smattered with some foreshadowing thrown in for good measure. The signs, those mileposts you look for, had been passing me by. My eyes were blind to the future. I didn't realize that my entire life had been preparing me to take on the odyssey of Parkinson's.

CLAP—Christmas Light Addiction Problem

I opened my eyes and BAM! It was 2:07 a.m., and no doubt about it, I was awake. It would soon be 2010, a new decade. Michael J. Fox would close his fundraiser promos with, "Let's cure Parkinson's within a decade." I was positive I was awake. (Trouble sleeping is another one of those symptoms you don't hear much about.) I went downstairs and turned on the TV. I thought maybe it would be nice to find some movies of Christmas lights. So, I searched YouTube and found a Trans-Siberian Orchestra song playing and the lights on the house were blinking and flashing in step to the music!

"Cool," I thought.

There was "All I Want for Christmas," "Jingle Bells," "Carol of the Bells," Manheim Steamroller, Mariah Carey, Muppets, and Josh Grobin. Then I clicked on "Amazing Grace." The entire home was covered. The lights flashed a single color over the entire house—the yard, shrubs, trees, and everything.

Red. Green. White. The lights looked as if they were spinning around the tall tree. It was beautiful. After just over a minute, it was done. I stumbled onto the work of a lighting legend, Richard Holdman's Utah home. Thousands and thousands of lights. He created a unique star topper, and it became known as the Holdman Star. These were thirty-, fifty-, and one-hundred-count light strings. Each string was a single color. So, to do red, green, clear, and blue, you needed four strings. Four times the string width. Four times the weight. Four times the—YIKES—electrical load. I had to learn more about this. I downloaded the video and showed it to anyone who would view it. I was looking for opinions. All that work for one song. One song! I was about to enter the bright, shiny world of the Christmas decorator. A lightshow guy. I studied up on lights, controllers, channels, Renard, pigtails, zip ties, the portable hole, and extension cords.

I knew some things about electricity. Don't stick a screwdriver in socket. Stay away from puddles. The fuse box is in the garage. I also learned that if you saw snow melt by your extension cords, that wasn't good.

I jumped in and purchased a preassembled controller. A brand-new D-light 16. She was beautiful. She had pigtails too. Now to find the software. I thought it was called Vixen. Whoa! Better be careful when typing vixen into a search box. You could get something totally different than software. What was left? I had a problem. Where did you get Christmas lights in June? How would I know how many to get? What should I put them on? How would I get the cords under the sidewalk? Better yet how would I get them out of the garage? I wondered if there was a blog out there.

As we moved into September, questions had answers, but the to-do list was growing. I was doing a live show vs. a single-tree, internet only. I would use seven fresh-cut trees from Home Depot. I would set up Thanksgiving week. I would do a press release the week before Thanksgiving. I would need about six thousand lights and sixteen extension cords. I would need voiceovers. I needed to test the controller. I was told to watch my amps on each circuit. What was an amp?

September moved into October. Complicating matters was that I could only do the physical parts of the show on weekends, as I was commuting from Orlando. There were five weeks until the first show. I conducted my first full outdoor test. I used high kitchen chairs as my trees. My daughter was here with the grandkids. I hit the start button and walked out of the garage. As I stepped out of the garage, I heard, "Let's get ready to RUMBULLLLLLLE!" The lights were alternating left-side/right-side in perfect sync with the beat. My daughter and her kids burst out laughing!

Perfect reaction.

Before I knew it, the time for setup had arrived. Snow had entered the picture. It was more difficult, but I forged ahead.

• • •

The trees looked great. The lights were spectacular. It was fun to watch cars drive up and stay. *The Minneapolis Star Tribune* did a cover-page story on the display. Plymouth Cable News sent out a reporter to get some behind-the-scenes coverage. On Christmas Eve I received a call from a reporter who wanted to feature the display and my story. He spent two hours with me. The report ran on the 6:00 p.m. and 10:00 p.m. news slots. I had done it. This guy who only a few years earlier didn't even want to tell his family he had Parkinson's now literally was announcing to the entire world he had the disease. However, this was just the beginning.

The reporter did take one liberty: he told the world that next year's display would be bigger and better.

Trust No One

I was still a commuter to my Orlando office. The weekly flights had begun to extract a toll on my body. Worse yet the fatigue I was suffering from began to take a toll on my accuracy. Numbers presented that were wrong and couldn't be trusted were useless. As 2012 drew to a close, I made the decision to accept my fate, and after consulting with my family, neurologist, and employer, I retired on disability on December 31, 2012. With my retirement I started the process of completing forms. Then came my first surprise. Insurance companies lie, use delay tactics, and even try to change the rules before they send you your check. They knew that once they accepted my diagnosis, they would have to pay me for ten years. That was $231,600!

Now that sounds like I should fly off to Tahiti, but that amount would equal only 65% of my pre-disability salary when added to Social

Security. I would not receive a lump sum but monthly payments until I was sixty-five.

Denied. That was the first response to the submission of my claim with the private carrier. They requested I supply additional documentation. They asked to see the acceptance letter from Social Security.

That was just plain wrong. I had a copy of the policy. Nowhere was it in print that that was required. They knew (a) it took five months for the Social Security Administration (SSA) to review your claim and (b) the folks at SSA were just like the insurance people and had a terrible track record on approving Parkinson's disability claims. In fact, the insurance company policy stated they would help me get approval from SSA and not the other way around. It took a letter from a lawyer on his letterhead inquiring as to the location of the text requiring SSA approval and pointing out that my application appeared to be in order, fulfilling all requirements. Bada-bing, bada-boom! I had a check in hand just days later with no mention of prior requests, just the benefit check.

Social Security was next. I researched the Social Security Administration's Blue Book. This book was the definitive resource to define an ailment or illness. The Parkinson's definition was short, barely twenty-one words in two paragraphs. The key for me was the requirement for two limbs to be affected. The letter from my neurologist explained just that. I was down to the final step, an interview and exam by their in-house doctor. I refrained from taking my Parkinson's medication so there could be no doubt about my abilities. He gave the usual commands: twist hands at wrists, tap on the floor, repeat the last three items in the list when I ask. Then a question took me by surprise.

"How far can you walk?"

"Uh—I don't know—I guess about a mile."

"A MILE!?!"

Whoop! Red alert. Whoop. Red alert. Whoop. Wrong answer.

"Well, I mean not very fast…"

. . .

I thought for sure that I had blown it, but no—I was approved. Only three in ten are approved on the first try, and I made it. The absolute key is to apply the blue book definition to yourself. Don't stretch your symptoms to fit it. Fatigue, no matter how relevant, is a hard line to cross. If your other symptoms fit the definition, leave fatigue out.

I was lucky, even with the shenanigans the insurance carrier pulled. Tack on disability insurance if at all possible. Through an employer the group plan is relatively cheap. If you can pay for the premiums. If you do then the benefits are tax-free. Check the policy language for preexisting conditions. Sometimes there is a period of time stated that clears the preexisting condition. Probably a year. In other words, you join the plan. You have been diagnosed with Parkinson's. One year after the join-in date, your condition is cleared, and you may now qualify.

RETURN OF CLAP

Each of the three seasons that followed were indeed bigger and better. We escalated from 8,000 to 20,000 and then to 40,000 lights. I continued to get generous news coverage. Each year I created a new hook. One year I played a Wii guitar that controlled lights in real time. As I was working full time, it was challenging. As I said earlier, in 2013, that had changed.

Retirement meant I could invest all my time into the production, which I referred to as PD Shimmers. It began to consume me. I was investing in my passion. My neurologist, Dr. Nance, commented, "All I have to do is say the words light show, and your entire demeanor changes." I straightened up and smiled.

Passion Compulsion

The year 2014 would be a breakout year. There were Parkinson's light tour buses. They included a favors box and carolers performing on the bus between stops. There was a Parkinson's setup day so everyone could take pride in the display. Each of the eight homes in Ithaca were part of the show. The show grew to 58,000 lights. It's a significant number as 58,000 Americans are diagnosed with Parkinson's each year.

We showcased that number. The display would start dark as the announcer told the audience that we would ramp all lights to full-on, a rarity in shows because of the electrical draw. As lights hit full-on, the announcer continued, "We shine one light for each American diagnosed with Parkinson's disease this year."

Show visitors approached me.

"Let me shake your hand."

"Thank you!"

"Thank you for what you do."

"I was diagnosed three years ago. What you do is amazing. Thank you."

A letter sent in said, "Your lightshow and Parkinson's work is phenomenal." And another said, "I was diagnosed last year, and now I have new hope."

Then I opened this one.

"Last year I was one of your lights. Depressed with my diagnosis, my wife suggested we come to see your show. When all the lights were lit and were 'shimmering,' I realized I was not alone. Thank you."

"All Lights" was the most popular sequence I had ever done. I never dreamed I would get the responses I did. A car drove in from Duluth (that's a three-and-a-half-hour drive—each way) because their mother had Parkinson's, and they wanted her to see what could be accomplished in spite of it.

We took donations using red boxes located in the center of the display. Children would walk hand in hand with Dad or Mom to put their donation in the slot.

We added greeters to help control traffic. More and more people looked for me so they could say thanks.

To top it off, my story was featured on the very popular news segment "Land of 10,000 Stories."

We also were recognized as a "Best in Twin Cities."

The following spring, I was told I would be honored for my work in the Greater Midwest area and would receive The Paul M. Silverstein Award. Dr. Nance would present it to me.

Plymouth's mayor appeared for seven years in a row on the Monday after Thanksgiving to officially kick off the display. It was known as Mayor's Night. It was a social event for my neighborhood. A sort of peace offering to thank the neighbors for the chaos that was upcoming.

I decided to use the greeters to collect donations. As a crutch they offered cookies. Who doesn't love cookies? So, we added Parkinson's cookies night. We handed out fifty dozen cookies.

There were Parkinson's song dedications. KSTP TV ABC Minneapolis did live news cut-ins. WCCO TV CBS Minneapolis Mornings reported live from the display. It was a little funny to see the neighborhood all lit up at 4:30 a.m.

One Saturday a guy called out to me, "Hey, have you looked at Google Maps? You're on it!"

Sure enough—under traffic. The entire Twin Cities map was green except for a three-block section on Ithaca Lane that was solid red. I didn't just have a hit; I had a bona fide success on my hands.

The compliments continued,

"You are doing God's work."

"Bless you!"

In year ten I approached a car and asked if this was their first time at the display.

"No, we come every year. We haven't missed a single year." There were three kids in the car. They looked to be about seven, nine, and ten or eleven. I had become a Christmas tradition for this family. I was touched by that thought.

This was more than a compulsive act originating as a medicinal side effect; it was a deep passion.

That summer Karen and I attended a wedding. At the reception there were table leaders to help get people mingling. Ours started with, "Please tell us what your favorite music is."

Moving left to right, the answers chimed in.

"Pop."

"Rock."

"Jazz."

And when it was my turn, "Christmas."

After a few chuckles, Karen defended me.

"No, he is serious—it's Christmas."

The leader lady spoke, "Let's try again with this question. Ok, Mike, name a rapper."

"Cellophane," I quickly said.

She gave up.

The light show would peak in 2016. That December in Dr. Nance's office for my usual checkup, I proclaimed, "Last week I logged 27,644 steps on Saturday."

She replied, "YOU WHAT?"

"My Fitbit says I did over 27,000 steps. I even missed a dosage by an hour and a half and never missed it!"

She went on, concerned, "You are not a twenty-eight-year-old anymore. You are fifty-nine. And have lived with Parkinson's for thirteen years. And dopamine—you only have so much. Those cells die every day. You can't push so hard."

She was right. It was getting harder to do, and it didn't help that I was a perfectionist.

The show continued to grow. We did live streaming webcasts. Video was projected on the garage door. We continued to experiment. Early one morning the *tilt-up* tree of lights began to tilt over its center point when a sustained fifty-mile-per-hour west wind hit at 5:00 a.m. I quickly gathered my sons to fight the wind and bring the lights down before the light pole could crack and ram the house. This isn't LA; it's Minnesota. The display had to endure the harsh conditions. Temperatures of minus twenty. Wind-driven snow. Snow depths of twenty inches. Controller boxes would be buried in ice and snow.

I had become an engineer, a computer geek, an electrician, a musician, a conductor, a videographer, a writer, an editor, and a marketing wiz. I was soldering electrical circuit boards. I was using skills learned from friends when I was ten years old. Ironically my soundtrack was broadcast on FM radio within a two-mile range. It was even better than WJJJ.

My ever-present persona continued welcoming cars to the show. Then one night—a surprise. A car pulled out of line and crossed over the center line. As I walked up to a window, a hand came out. It was my brother-in-law! He and his wife had flown in from Chicago as a surprise, and they were going to work as greeters. A few minutes later, a car pulled up, and another brother-in-law swung the door open and jumped out. He and his wife flew in from Charlestown, South Carolina. They all wanted to be a part of what I was doing.

I always worried about what the neighbors were thinking about what I did to their neighborhood. All I had to do was look around. It seemed houses with lights expanded each year. I would knock on a door to request if I could put a directional sign in an unknown neighbor's yard to help with traffic. I consistently heard the answer, "We love the light show. Glad to help!" I created a show voiceover: "An entire neighborhood supporting the Mike Justak Foundation for Parkinson's disease."

One person can indeed touch many lives. I cherished the myriad of letters. One contained a card with $4.62 in it. It was signed, "I love your lights! I love to help people smile."

I was ready to quit in 2017 when a neighbor offered to move the show to his home and the surrounding neighbors. He and his neighbors would ease the workload.

Most of the work still needed my expertise, and even with John, my apprentice, the work was even more demanding. Challenges were many. Higher traffic counts, street incline, forty-foot trees. The street was congested with full-size motor coaches, limos, and even a trolley. A single Sunday hour had 400 cars pass through. I moved it back to Ithaca in 2019, where it somewhat slimmed down.

Due to the 2020 pandemic, shows would only run via reserved time slots.

Then on December 27, 2021, standing beside all my neighbors and their children, I watched the lights shimmer one last time. At 9:02 p.m. PD Shimmers went dark permanently.

• • •

The money raised was used in a myriad of ways. Exercise was a top funding priority. Wii game systems were given as prizes. Exercise class sessions would drop user rates to just two dollars. Boxing therapy costs would be underwritten. Boxing gloves were supplied at little cost. Ice cream socials, rounds of golf, general support to the Struthers Parkinson's Center, bike maintenance, Parkinson's bus tours, the bus to Parkinson's Day at Twins Baseball—all of these were funded. That wasn't all though: thank you dinners for Parkinson's staff, yoga classes, Bombas socks, tables at award banquets, winter coats for greeters, Nordic walking poles, Peloton bike rides, money to fund research. All of this happened because one guy wasn't afraid to walk a path he didn't know. I invested my whole being in creating success. And my symptoms eased at times. Do what you love. Your life may just depend on it. Following a passion can motivate and give purpose. The sense of accomplishment may improve your emotional wellbeing. Engaging in activities that you are passionate about can relieve stress. You may recall that stress can exacerbate Parkinson's symptoms. Don't stand on the edge, jump in!

Reason

Do things really happen for a reason? Imagine if there never had been a PD Shimmers or if I hadn't contracted Parkinson's. It truly transformed me. Nineteen years. No one should have a disease they live with for twenty years. Parkinson's patients are real warriors. They arise each new day and prepare to do battle. What is the objective for today? What is it one seeks to accomplish? I'm not talking about save-the-world stuff. What is important is to set a goal and, at the end of day, measure to see if you accomplished it. What is your plan, General?

Are you ready to fight?

Get up! Move! Have hope. Fight back. Hope!

How? You need to employ ways to fight Parkinson's at every turn. To do this you need to attack it every day. Exercise your brain. Keep it engaged in life. Challenge it daily. Count to one hundred by threes. Count down from one hundred by threes or by threes plus two. Challenge your brain to multitask. Do drills. Dribble a ball. Now dribble and weave through a pylon course. Do the above and count as well. Keep the focus on hope.

Exercise every day. Start small and increase. Keep in mind that movement begets movement. Find the book *Delay the Disease* by David Zid. David has been teaching that exercises can reverse symptoms since before 2008. His methods work. Stretch. Walk. Run. Ballroom dance. Nordic walk. Spin. Row. Play Wii. Swim. Golf. Snowshoe. Shoot hoops. You have to move! Don't lose hope.

Look at who is near you—your inner circle, so to speak. Find people you trust who are willing to help, people who share a collective feeling of optimism, someone who can bring a smile to your face, someone who can champion even the smallest of accomplishments. For example, create a goal for the day each morning at eight o'clock. Write it down. You have already created a positive day because you have accomplished a task. Savor it. Revel in it. Today IS going to be great.

Look Up

Almost one in two people with Parkinson's suffer from depression. Don't spiral down but use your optimist friends to spiral up. You have to fight. It IS NOT easy. Today you move. Tomorrow, you feel better, so you move again. The pattern repeats to spiral up.

Find optimism in your day. Smile as you walk through a corridor of people. Look at the people looking at you. Optimists will smile back, while others will ponder, "What's so funny?"

Is your glass half full? Your support circle will keep you on track. Keep trying. Look for those who inspire you, who challenge you. Don't say impossible. You see even the word impossible itself screams optimism, as it says I'm possible. Hope!

Laugh

Part of your daily challenge is how you look at your situation. A sense of humor can go a long way to help you when things don't go right. The situations you may find yourself in can be quite funny. Your freezing gait might kick in as you cross the path of a member of the opposite sex. Embarrassed you stand and proclaim, "Better be careful, or you may fall for me, as it appears I have fallen for you." I have a favorite video clip that makes me laugh every time I see it. It is from the animated series *Family Guy*. The scene references Michael J. Fox as a mistaken Zorro replacement. The joke is based on the line from Zorro. Who was that man? I don't know, but he left his insignia. The camera pans to the wall to see a scribbled mess as opposed to the sharp-lined Z.

Has anyone told you the secret that is attached to Parkinson's? Parkinson's makes you better looking. No, really. Prior to my diagnosis,

I would travel and go to meetings seemingly unnoticed. Now when I approach, I hear the person almost gleefully exclaim, "Wow! Mike—you look great!" I never heard that before Parkinson's. You just go with the flow. Use your Parkie vocabulary to inject a bit of humor. Favorite drink? Milkshake. Song? Shake it Off. Music group? The Tremors. Basketball player? Shake Key O'Neill. Martini? Shaken, not stirred.

"Hey, Bill! You must be a real outgoing guy."
"Why?"
"I always see you shaking hands."
Ooo, that's a bad one.

PLAN

It also becomes more important than ever to plan. If you are an early-onset patient or not, you still should review your financial plan. Have you considered disability insurance? It may not be too late, even if you are diagnosed. Check the fine print in a policy for preexisting conditions. There may be a stated way to overturn the condition as preexisting. For example, you were diagnosed on May 1. You enroll on June 1. Your preexisting condition would disqualify you. Read the policy. It may contain override language.

Also be prepared for the unexpected. Social Security does not kick in until after five months have passed from your application date. Medicare is twenty-four months after your Social Security date. Then the unfortunate fact is that 60% of applicants with Parkinson's disease are denied their disability claim on the first try. Know the *blue book* definition of Parkinson's disease. Your application needs to *talk to* that definition.

What do you plan to do when you retire? What have you always wanted to do? Where does your passion lie? You can turn that passion into therapy. Staying connected keeps your brain engaged. It offers challenges. It forces you to keep moving. It helps you create goals. So, give sincere thought to what you wish to do. If you don't have knowledge on the subject, find a mentor. Use Google to research. Learn what you need to know. Just Do It!

And remember to create and nurture that passion. Involve your entire being. What is that one thing you have always wanted to do? Keep up hope.

It only needs one, you. Here is a great example. A guy who travels to many big cities around the globe becomes enamored by street performers. Street performers. They play, sing, or dance. If you like you put some change in the hat. The guy is inspired and records a performance of "Stand by Me." He then goes to a second street performer and records him as the street performer listens to playback. The process repeats, and he finds street performers in Amsterdam, St. Petersburg, and even in Africa. From a simple idea to a passion, "Playing for Change" has raised millions of dollars to build schools that teach the arts as well as life skills. One person—one. Take a look at John Lennon's "Imagine," performed by Playing for Change. Yoko Ono even granted rights for Playing for Change to use it. Find it on YouTube.

Did Freud Live in Hollywood?

What if your life were a twentieth century movie? What movie would it be?

The Blues Brothers, *It's a Wonderful Life*, *2001: A Space Odyssey*.

These three embody the most important aspects of my life. The circular path events take.

They all deal with themes of hope and redemption. In *2001: A Space Odyssey*, Dave Bowman is transformed by his encounter with the monolith, and he ultimately achieves a state of pure being. In *The Blues Brothers*, Jake and Elwood redeem themselves by saving the orphanage where they were raised. And in *It's a Wonderful Life*, George Bailey is shown what life would have been like if he had never been born, and he realizes that his life has had a positive impact on the world.

They all have a lasting impact. *2001: A Space Odyssey* is considered to be one of the greatest science fiction films ever made. *The Blues Brothers* is a cult classic that has been praised for its music, humor, and action sequences. And *It's a Wonderful Life* is a Christmas classic that continues to be enjoyed by audiences of all ages.

Despite their differences these three films all share a common thread: they are all about the power of hope and redemption. They are all stories about people who find the strength to overcome adversity and make a difference in the world.

How about you?

HOPE

Remember to HOPE to feel better. Have at least a piece of HOPE each day. Think of it this way. Have an elevated sense of humor. When you progress through your day, smile and be optimistic. Create, prepare, or follow through with a plan or jump in headfirst to follow a passion. Don't just sit; you have to move. Exercise is the key. Got it now?

Humor

Optimism

Plan (Passion)

Exercise

Use hope to help improve yourself and even inspire others to win with Parkinson's. It is a journey one wouldn't necessarily choose. Stay in an optimist's circle. Drive everyone you know crazy with your passion. Your journey may just inspire another. Don't stop there. Go ahead, make it an odyssey!

About the Author

Mike Justak, an inspiring public figure. Despite retiring on disability, he founded the Mike Justak Foundation for Parkinson's disease and has served as its President and Executive Director. With unwavering resilience, Mike draws strength from his 40-year marriage, four children, and five grandchildren. He showcased his creativity through PD Shimmers, an enchanting holiday light show synchronized to music, earning the prestigious "Best in Twin Cities" title for multiple years. Recognized with the Paul M Silverstein Community Service Award, Mike's remarkable dedication to the Greater Midwest Parkinson's Community continues to inspire countless others.